Things that I can't say at SCHOOL because I TEACH THERE

DO NOT I digest MANAGER

Parents: THE NIGHTMARE of my dreams

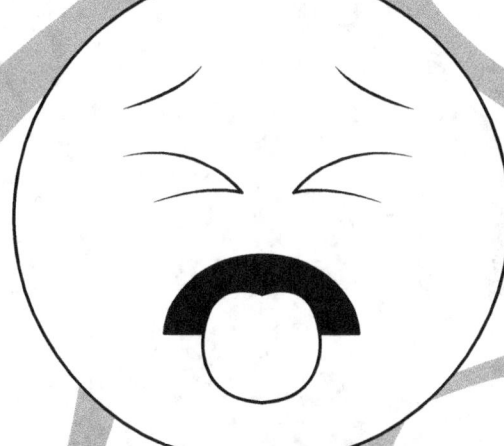

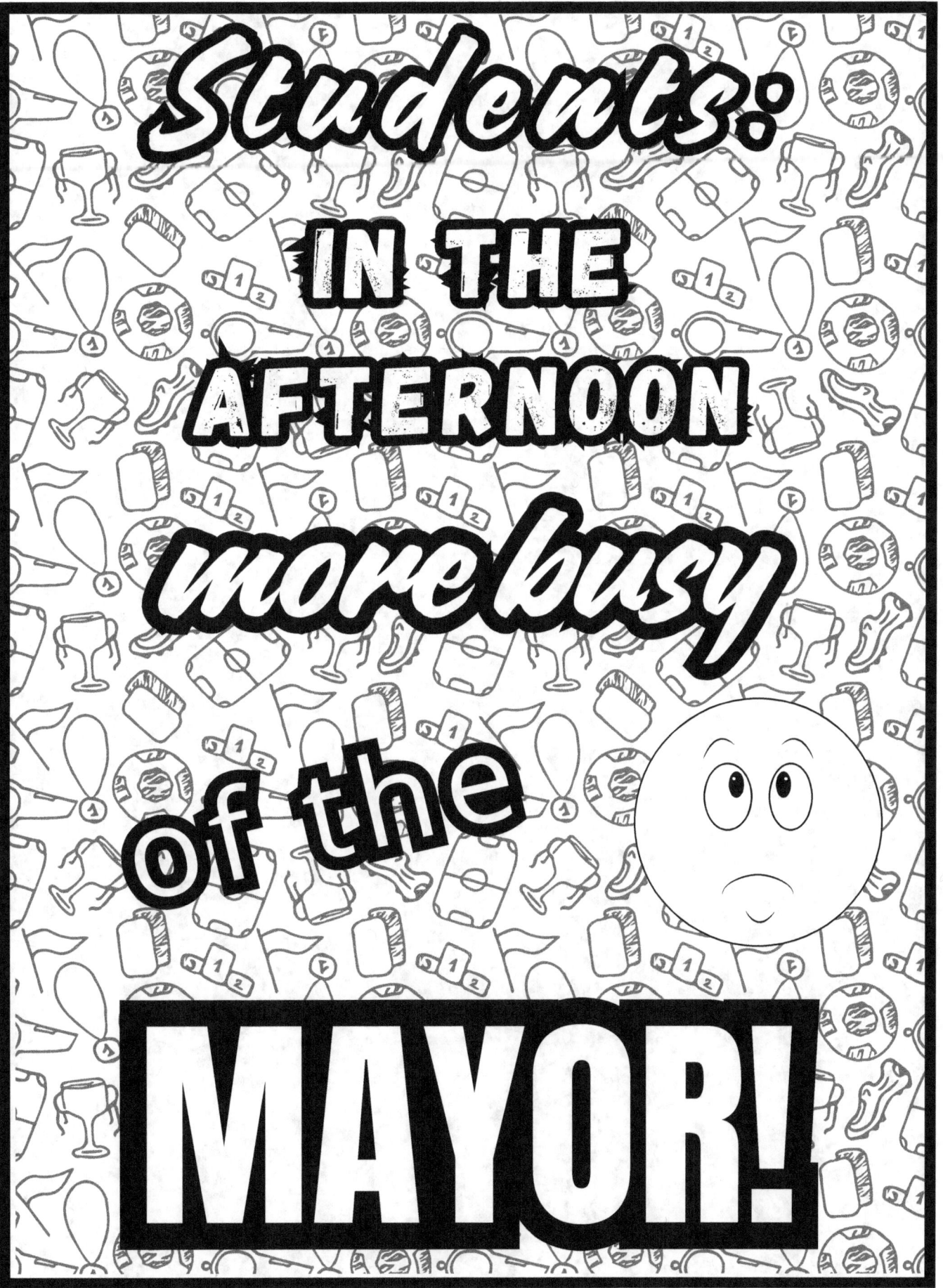

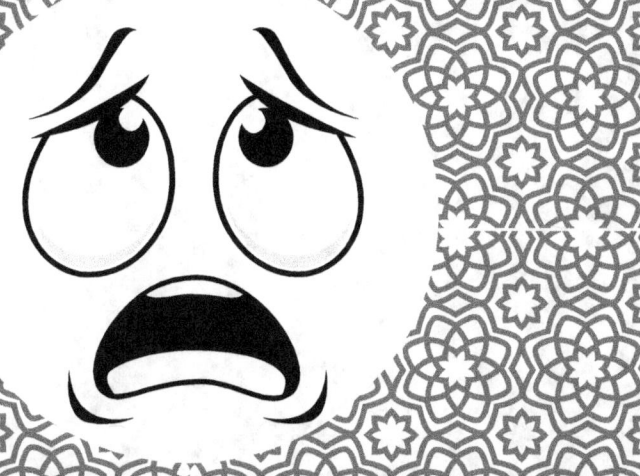

Colleagues: A CIRCUS without TENT

Students: Like Puppets with Batteries

Parents: as the SEVEN PLAGUES of Egypt

Colleagues: SPIES and ENVIOUS

MANAGER a LIGHTHOUSE without LIGHT

Students: DONKEYS with MOBILE PHONE

Parents: HARPIES looking for PREY

Online colleagues: can you hear me?

DO YOU SEE ME??

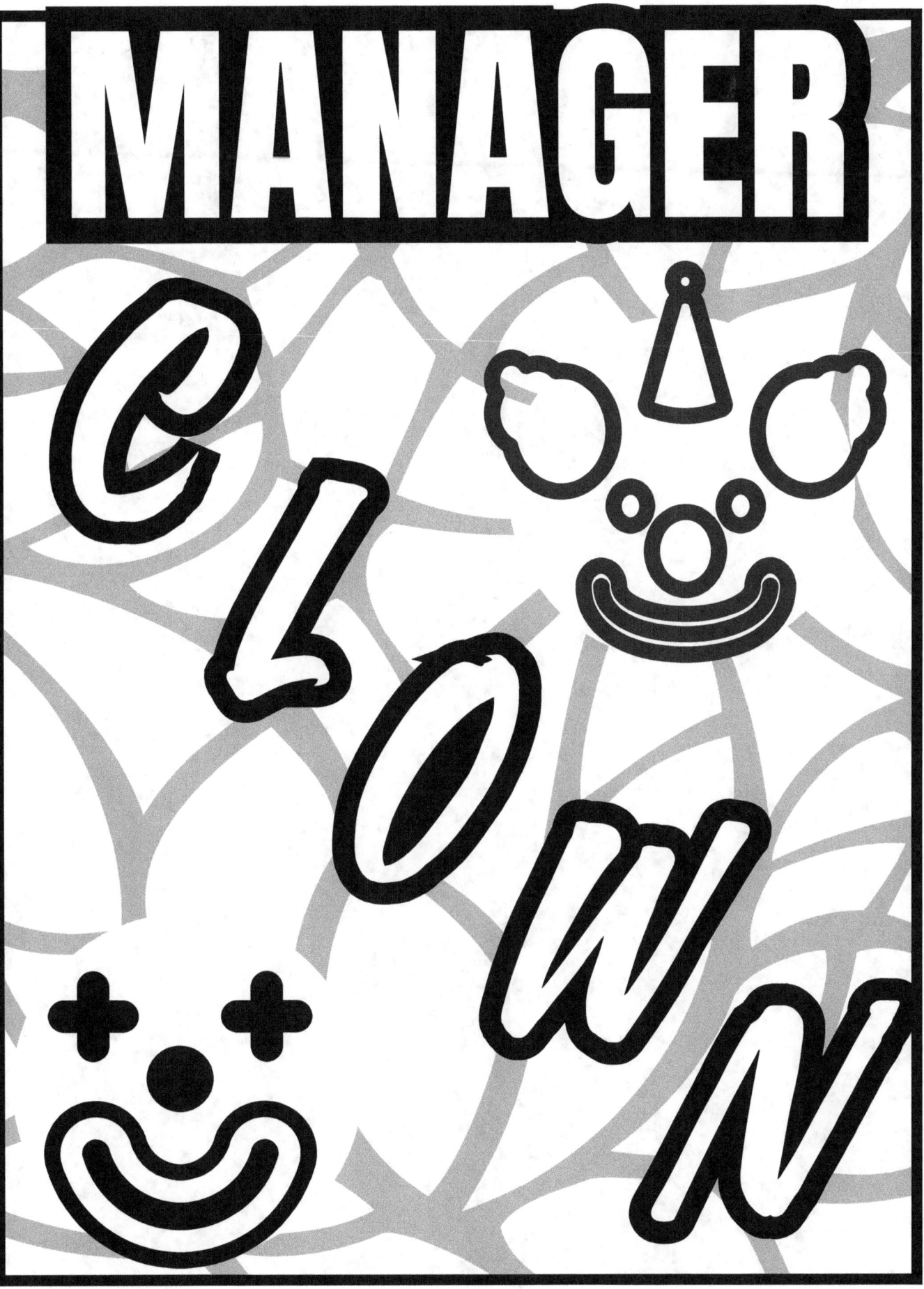

Students: SERIAL COPIERS

Parents: OUT OF SCHOOL!

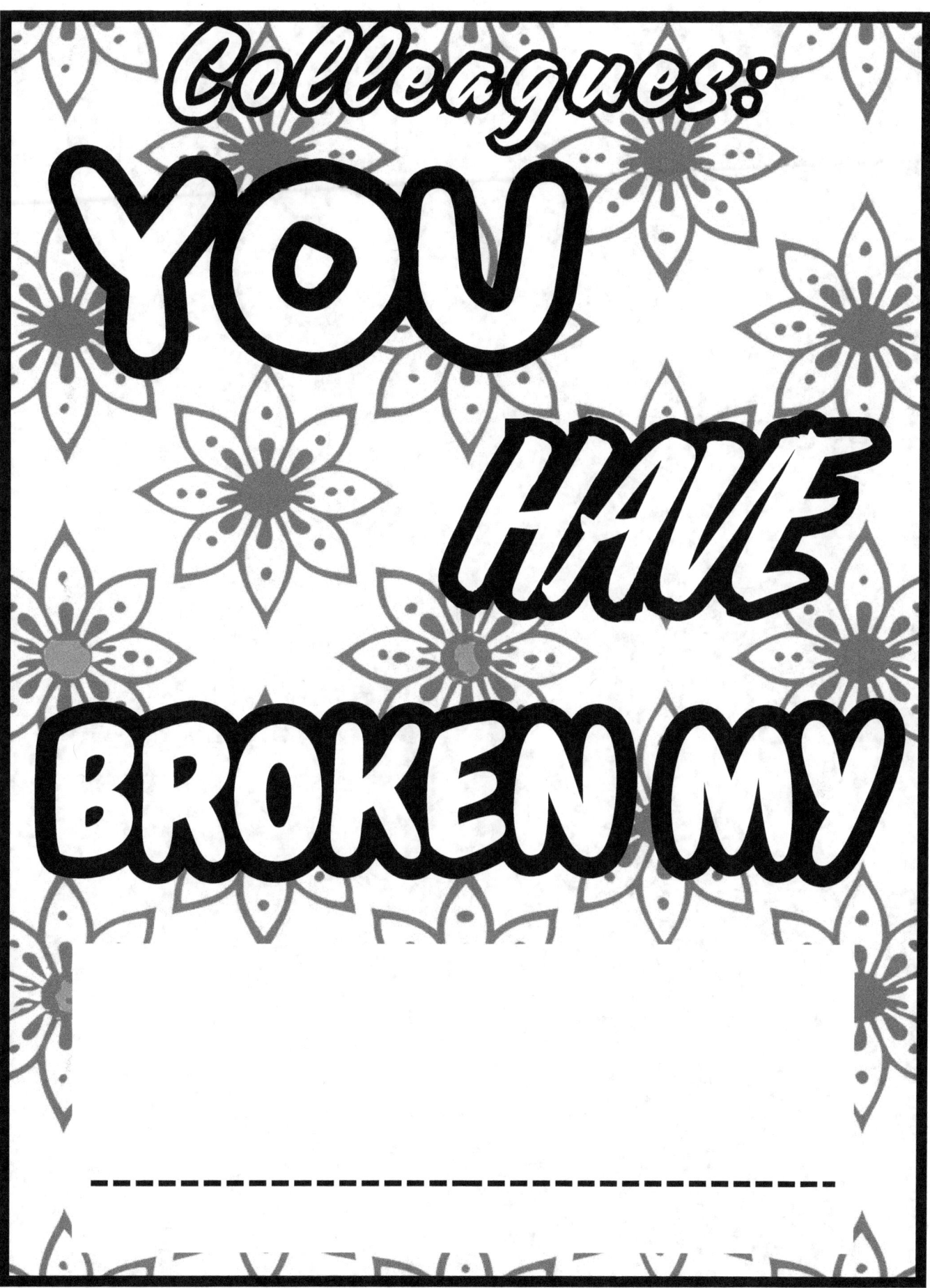

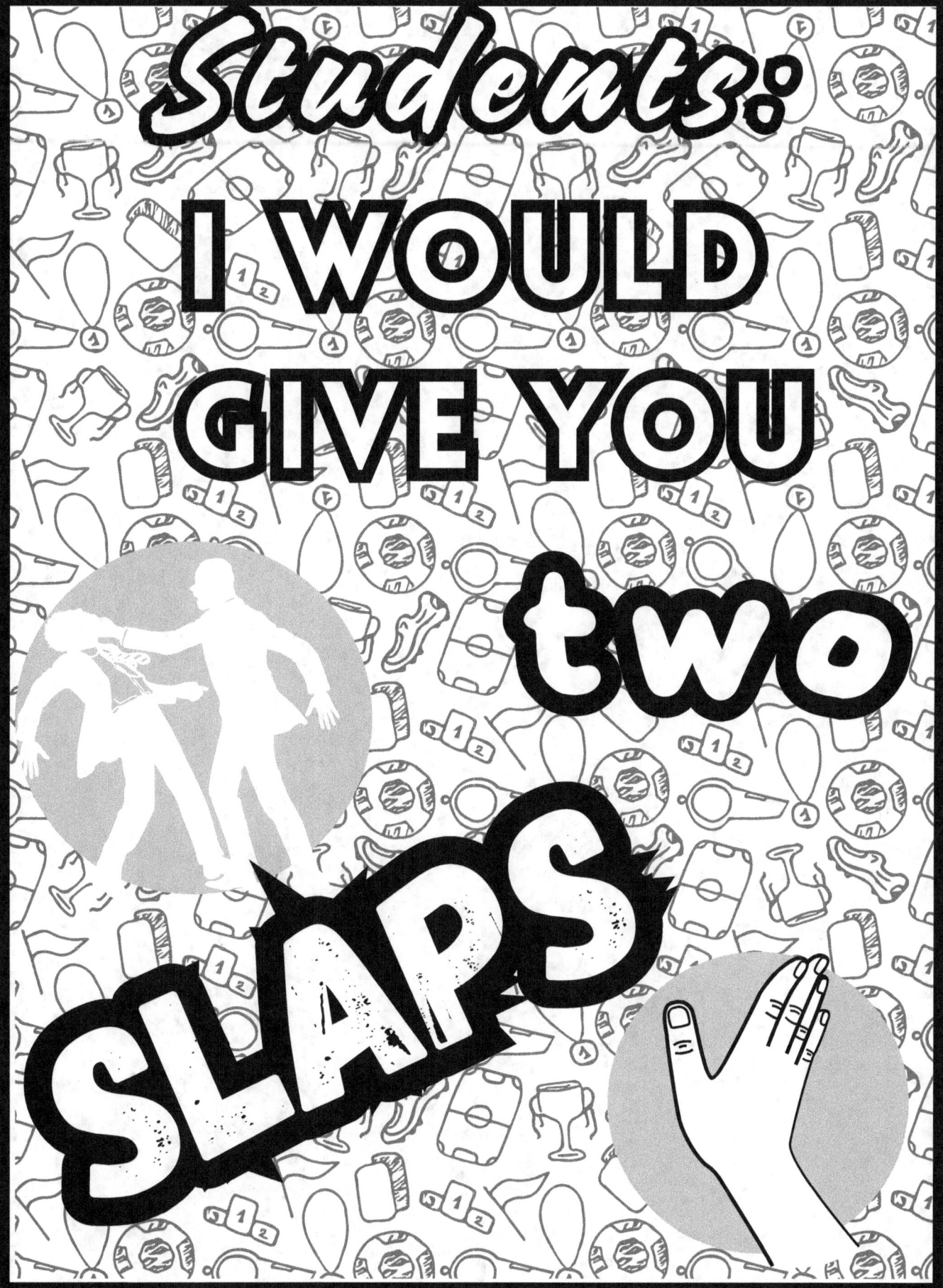

MANAGER ...BUT... have you seen yourself?

YOURSELF?

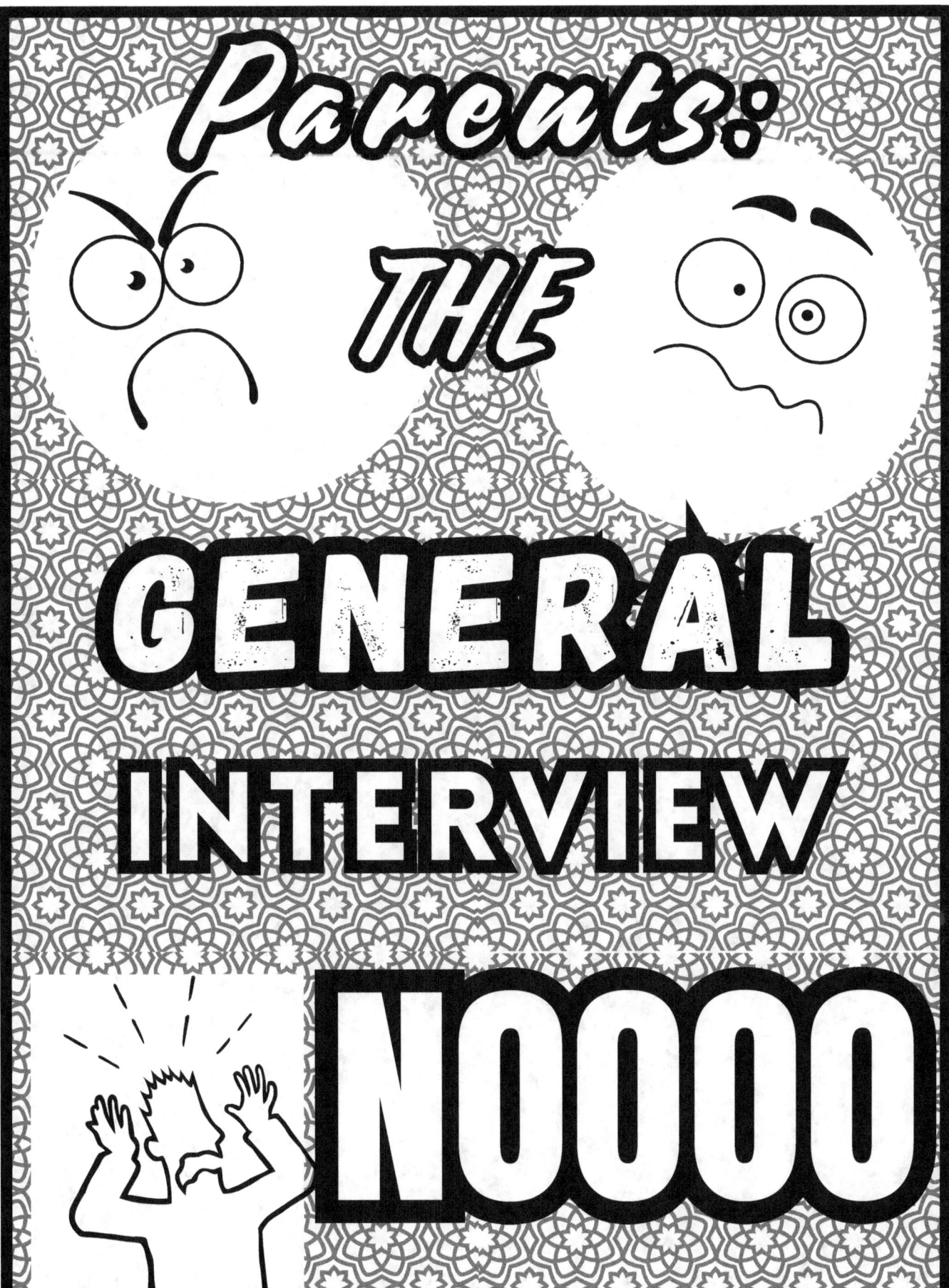

MANAGER

YOU ARE A BASTARD

Colleaugue BUT... how do you DRESS??

MANAGER:

CHANGE JOB!

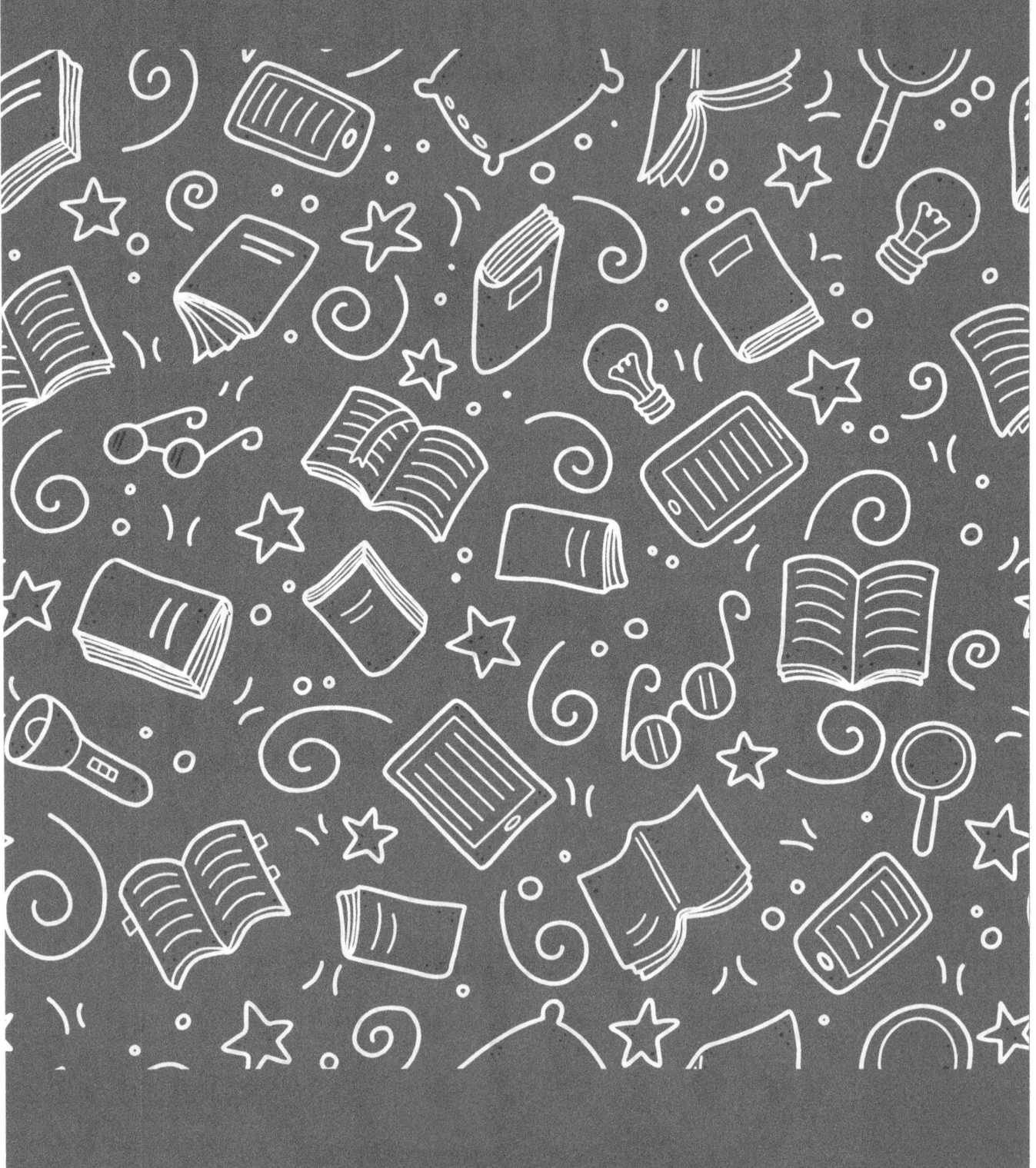

Parent: DO YOU WANT to teach instead ME?